Get to Know the Chemistry of Colors

Children's Science & Nature

There are many colors all around us. How does a compound show a certain color when you shine light on it?

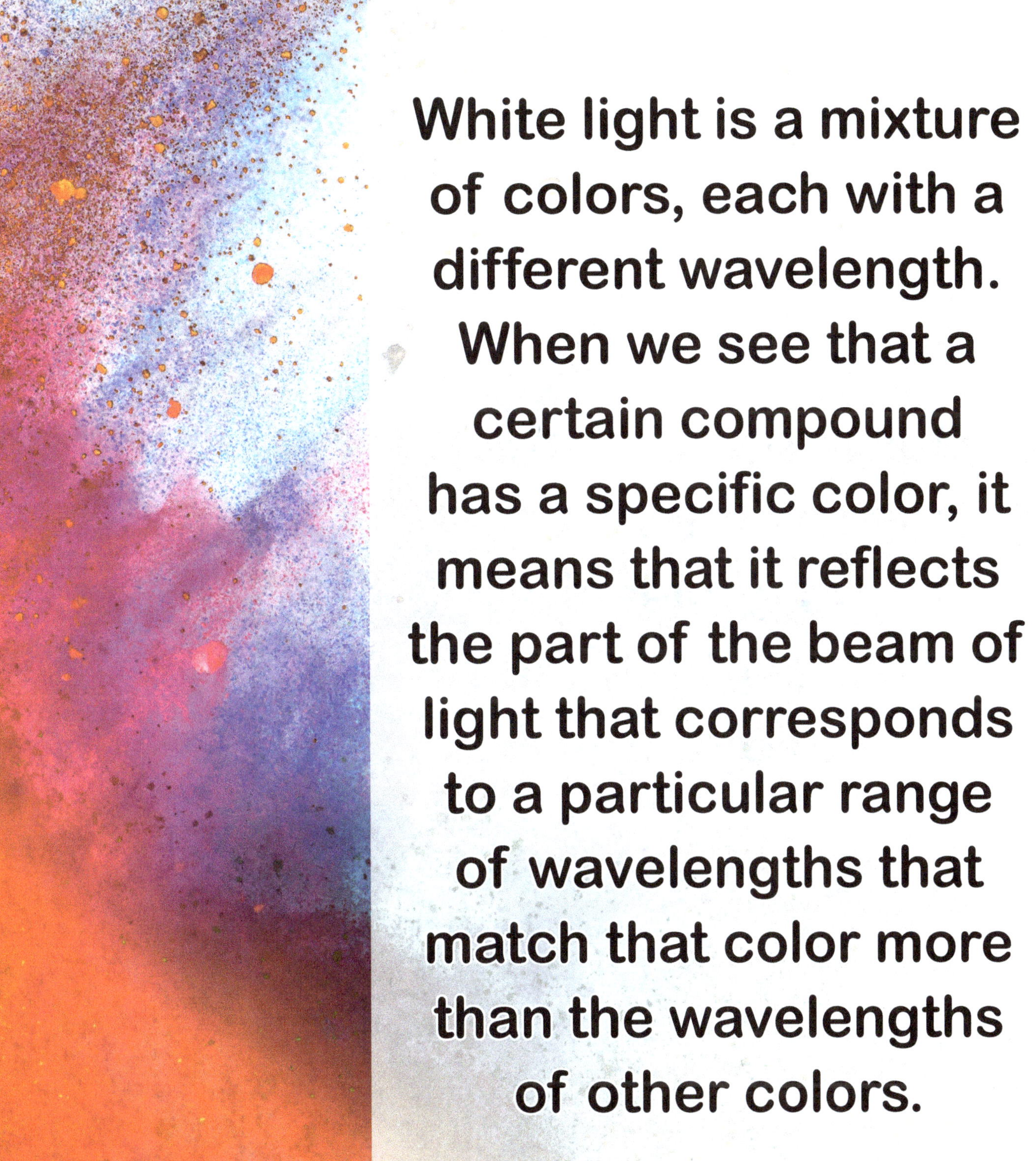

White light is a mixture
of colors, each with a
different wavelength.
When we see that a
certain compound
has a specific color, it
means that it reflects
the part of the beam of
light that corresponds
to a particular range
of wavelengths that
match that color more
than the wavelengths
of other colors.

Our eyes can only see the colors of the molecules that reflect light in the visible range.

Most organic compounds reflect ultraviolet (UV) light, but we can't see that range so they appear white to us. But these compounds look colorful to other creatures, such as bees, which can detect UV.

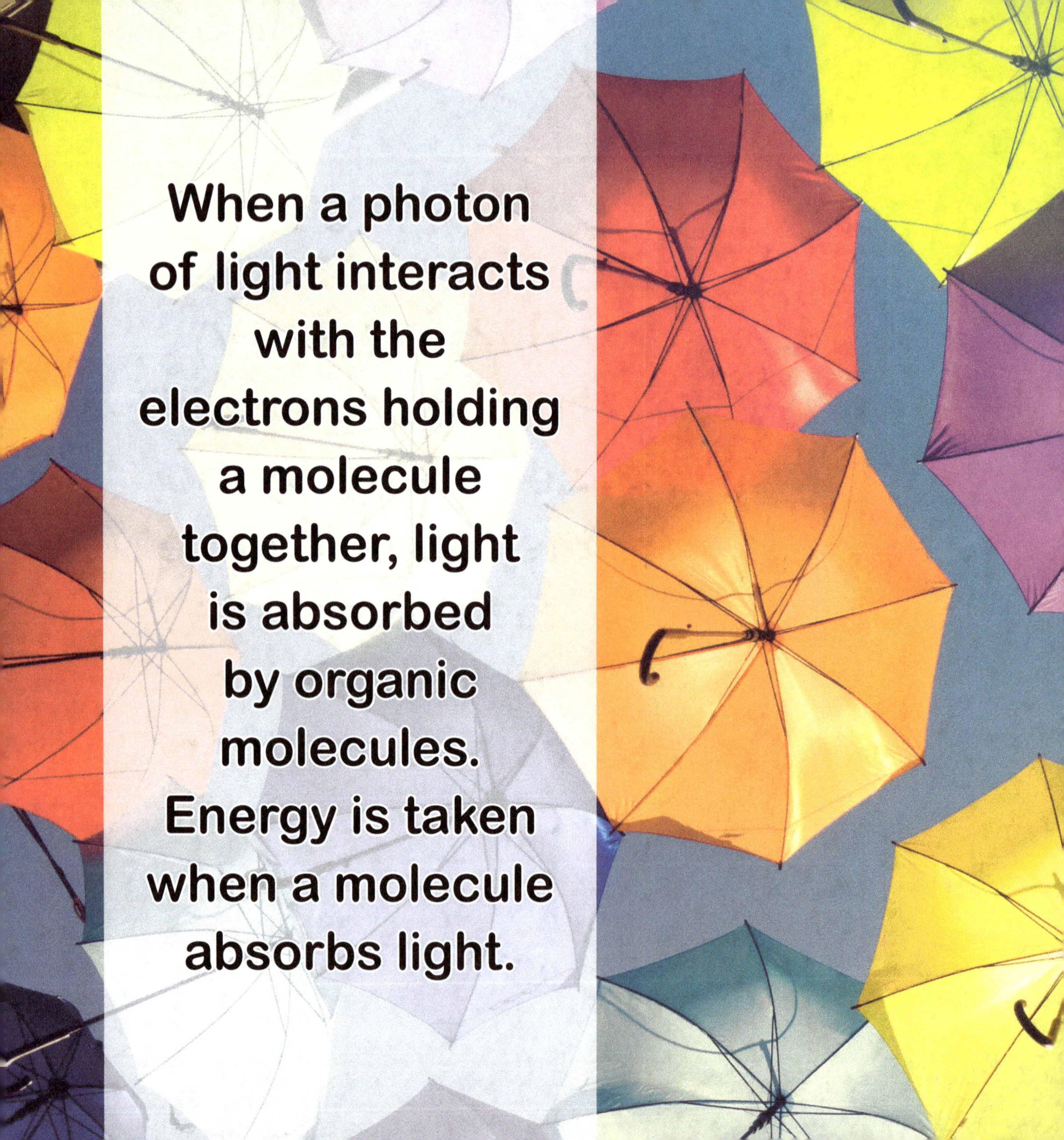
When a photon
of light interacts
with the
electrons holding
a molecule
together, light
is absorbed
by organic
molecules.
Energy is taken
when a molecule
absorbs light.

Because the energy content of a photon depends on its color, various electrons can be knocked out by varied colors of light, based on how tightly those electrons are bound into the molecule.

Red photons have the least energy, then followed by the green colored photons, the blue, and finally the violet photons that have the most energy in the visible light range. The ultraviolet photons even have more energy. X-rays are photons that have so much energy that we don't call them light any more.

There are a few particularly common molecular structures which have electrons in the right range of binding strength. These are the ones used for the families of dyes.

By changing the
atoms arranged
around the
active center, the
binding strength
— and thus the
color — can
be tuned to the
visible spectrum.

Indigo is one of the first natural dyes and famously puts the blue in jeans. Its color is derived from a set of three double-bonds in its center (O=C, C=C, C=O). Electrons can migrate in these double bonds when hit by the right amount of energy that corresponds to orange light.

Tartrazine is one of the synthetic food colorants for the garish hues of candies. The nitrogen double bond (N=N) in its middle gives rise to its bright orange color.

A persistent problem with many organic dyes such as tartrazine and indigo is that they are not light-fast. They fade over time due to the fact that they absorb much of the energy of visible light rather than reflecting, deflecting, or entirely ignoring it.

This means that they are prone to be damaged by that very light. Their color originates from delicate chemical structures and thus is gone when those structures are broken.

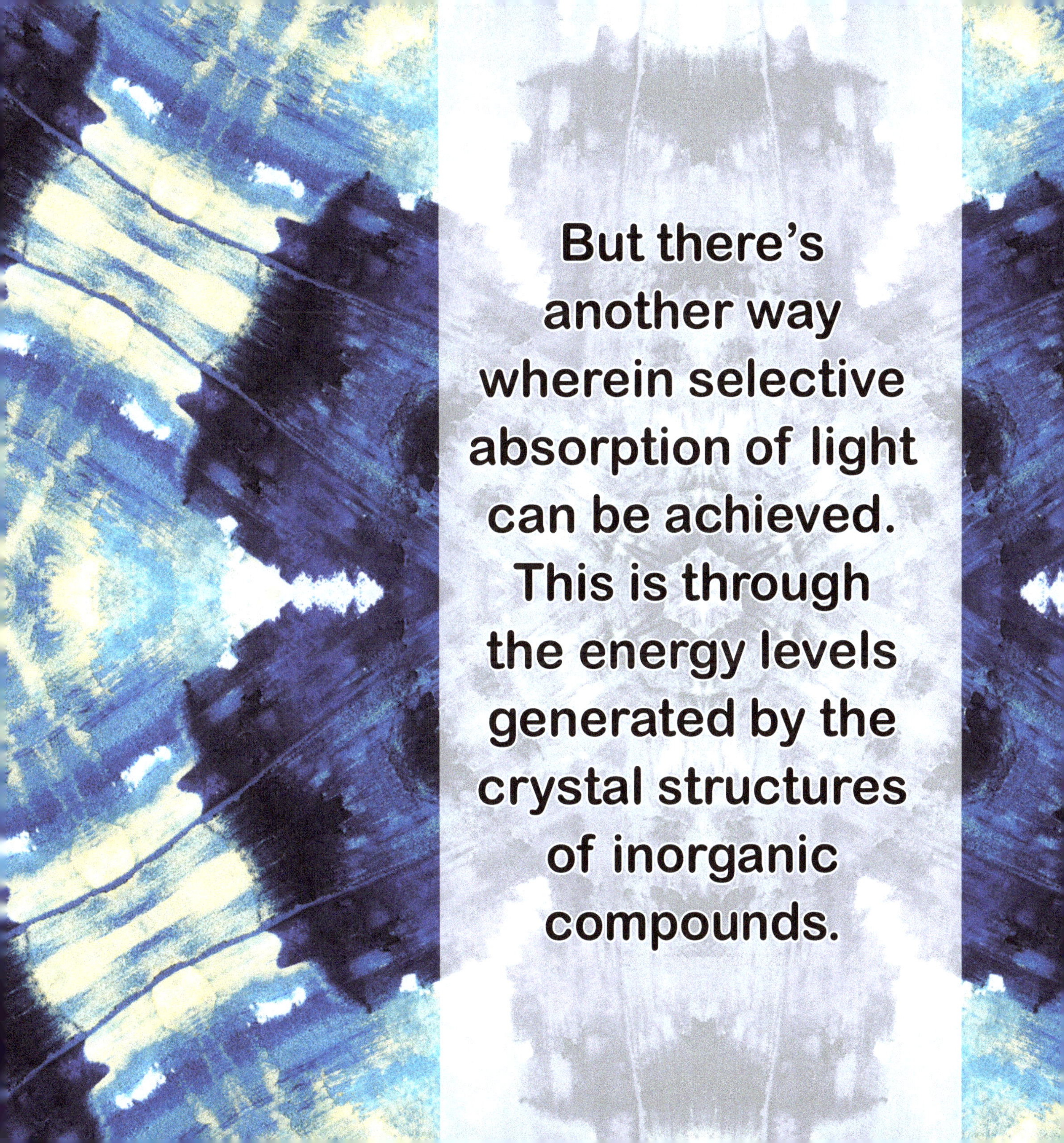

But there's another way wherein selective absorption of light can be achieved. This is through the energy levels generated by the crystal structures of inorganic compounds.

The Color of Crystals are forever

The first pigments like ochre are light-fast. These are still visible in the cave paintings done by early humans.

These inorganic
pigments were
based on a
crystalline
structure called
iron oxide which
is commonly
known as rust.
Ochre, the lightest
color, is almost
pure iron oxide.

Varying amounts of magnesium oxide (MgO) mixed with iron oxide give rise to sienna and the chocolaty umbra.

There is more to
know about colors
in chemistry.
Research more
and have fun.

Visit
BABY PROFESSOR
EDUCATION KIDS
www.BabyProfessorBooks.com
to download Free Baby Professor eBooks
and view our catalog of new and exciting
Children's Books

9 798869 443557